Step-*by*-Step
BEAD CARDS

KATE MACFADYEN

GUILD OF MASTER CRAFTSMAN PUBLICATIONS

First published 2005 by
Guild of Master Craftsman Publications Ltd
166 High Street, Lewes
East Sussex, BN7 1XU

ISBN 1 86108 446 3

British Cataloguing in Publication Data

A catalogue record of this book is available from the British Library.

Managing Editor: Gerrie Purcell
Production Manager: Hilary MacCullum
Photographer: Anthony Bailey
Editor: Alison Howard
Designer: Rebecca Mothersole

Colour reproduction by AltaImage
Printed and bound in Singapore by Kyodo Printing

745.5941

Although care has been taken to
ensure that the imperial
measurements are true and
accurate, they are only conversions
from metric; they have been
rounded up or down to the nearest
$1/8$in, or to the nearest convenient
equivalent in cases where the
metric measurements themselves
are only approximate. When
following the projects, use either
the metric or the imperial
measurements; do not mix units.

CONTENTS

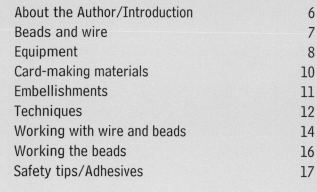

PROJECTS

ABOUT THE AUTHOR

Kate MacFadyen has always enjoyed crafts and is a highly qualified guide to the subject. Her hobbies include painting, cross stitch and making dolls' houses, plus the odd spot of gardening. She indulges her love of all things creative by working at a craft shop, where she also teaches card-making and wirecraft.

INTRODUCTION

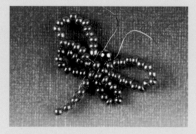

I discovered the technique of threading or 'knitting' beads to create interesting projects at the same time as I discovered wirecraft. I learned the technique from project books, but I decided to take it a step further. The craft is already popular in the US, where it is most often used for children's projects, including brooches, necklaces, hairclips and earrings. I decided to develop my own motifs that would be suitable for use in card-making. I tried a few of them out in one of the chapters of my first book 'Making Wirecraft Cards'.

Beads can be extremely addictive, and when you have made a few projects you will find yourself looking in craft shops and even second-hand shops for suitable beads. I hope you enjoy making these projects as much as I did.

Beads and wire

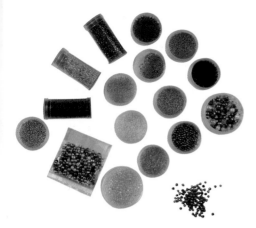

BEADS

Beads come in so many colours and sizes that you may soon be addicted to buying them! For cards, you can use tiny embroidery beads, seed beads, or larger beads measuring up to about 5mm (¼in) in diameter. Anything bigger will look too heavy in card projects.

There are so many pretty beads on the market, including a beautiful array of glass beads that lend themselves to special occasions. Try to find beads with a large hole in the middle. Some types of bead are coated with paint, which makes the hole so small that it is impossible to pass two pieces of wire through. The only way to use these beads is to enlarge the holes individually using a sewing needle, which is fiddly and time-consuming.

WIRE

Wire comes in a range of widths (gauges) and colours. Usually, the higher the number, the finer the wire. It must be fine enough to allow two strands to pass through the centre of each bead. For the projects in this book, I used 34- and 28-gauge wire. 28-gauge wire is available in a range of colours including gold, silver and rich copper, which I prefer because it is softer and more pliable. When you use tiny embroidery beads you will need 34-gauge wire, but for most of the other projects, 28-gauge is suitable. For any project, the larger the bead used, the longer the wire you will need. If you want to change any of the beads used in the projects for larger ones, adjust the length of wire accordingly.

Equipment

BASIC TOOL KIT

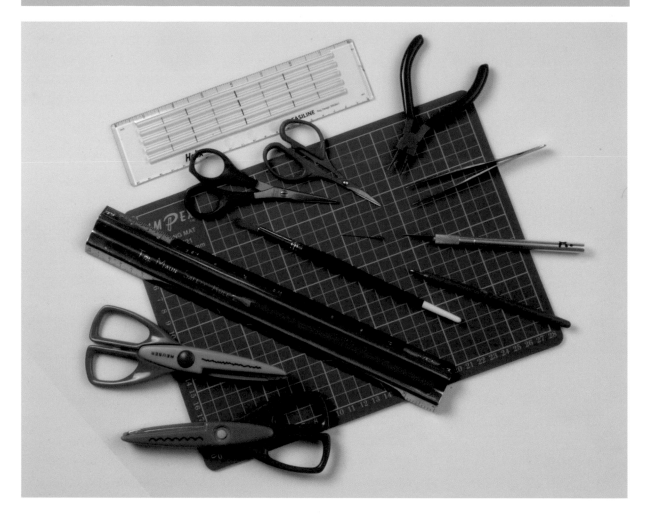

Cutting mat
The self-healing type is best, but you can also work on thick cardboard or folded scrap paper.

Ruler
Use a metal safety ruler, not a plastic or wooden ruler which may slip and cause accidents.

Scissors
Old scissors are ideal for cutting the wire, which is not so thick that it will need wire cutters. Small, sharp scissors are useful for cutting out card and paper.

Pliers
These are useful for various jobs, including cutting wire.

Tweezers
Pointed tweezers are invaluable for easing, pulling and pushing the wires through the beads.

Craft knife or scalpel
This is useful for making straight, precise cuts or trimming edges.

Pin
Use the point of a large pin or a needle to enlarge the holes of painted beads.

Fancy craft scissors
These are available in a range of designs to give the edge of your cards an attractive and professional touch.

Paintbrush
Use this when you are wet-tearing mulberry paper (see page 13).

Metal rule or straight edge
This is essential when cutting paper or card using a scalpel.

Embossing tool
Use this for embossing (see page 13) and to smooth along the folds of cards to give a clean finish.

Pencil
These are useful when measuring card and paper.

OTHER EQUIPMENT

Light box
This is an essential piece of equipment if you plan to do a lot of dry embossing.

Stencils
These are usually made of brass and are available in a wide range of designs. Use them with an embossing tool and light box.

Ink pads
These are available in a wonderful array of colours for use with rubber stamps.

Rubber stamps
These come in a wide range of designs, some quite intricate. They are ideal for decorating all kinds of greetings cards.

Decorative punches
Great fun to use, for card-making and general crafting.

Glitter glue
Adds an extra finishing touch to your cards.

Dimensional paint
Ideal for adding dots or for writing on your cards.

Card-making materials

CARD

You can buy card from craft shops or by mail order in a multitude of pretty colours to suit all occasions. The basic C6 card is 15 x 10cm (6 x 4in) when folded and fits most ready-made envelopes, or buy them to match if you prefer. Good-quality card is well worth the expense as it makes the finished project look more attractive and appealing. Cheaper card is useful for layering, rubber stamping, or for making decorative motifs and shapes.

DECORATIVE CARDS AND PAPERS

To complement your cards you need to invest in different coloured, textured and patterned cards and papers. They really add the finishing touch to a card.

Embellishments

One of the nicest things about making cards is adding embellishments. Ribbon, skeleton leaves, gemstones, punched flowers, tiny beads – the choice is endless. You will soon find that you have quite a collection of lovely things. Then the fun can really begin!

Tying bows

1 Form a loop between the forefinger and the thumb of one hand.

2 Form a second loop using your other hand.

3 Tie the two loops together as shown.

4 Gently pull the ends to form two equal-sized loops.

5 Pull the two loops tight again after readjusting.

6 Trim the ends to length.

Techniques

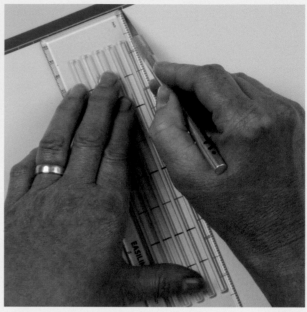

Using the mat, scalpel and ruler to cut a neat, straight edge

Using the mat, scalpel and ruler to cut card in half

Cutting on a mat

Scoring and folding card

CUTTING ON A MAT

Line up the top of the card with one of the lines on the mat. Press down firmly on the ruler, and cut the card with the point of the scalpel resting against the edge of the ruler.

SCORING AND FOLDING CARD

Line the top of the card with one of the lines on the cutting mat. Use an embossing tool to score the centre of the card, against the straight edge of the ruler. When the card has been scored, fold it in half neatly, matching the corners.

FOLDING CARD WITH A BONE FOLDER

This is optional, and can be used instead of, or after, folding the card with your fingers to give an added sharpness to the fold.

PUNCHING

To punch corners, line up the punch over the corner of your card, making sure that it sits centrally over the corner, and punch down with your fingers.

Using decorative scissors

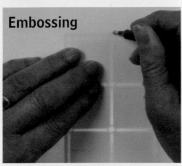

Embossing

Rubber stamping

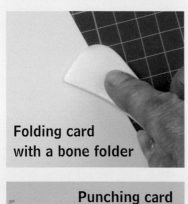

Folding card with a bone folder

Punching card

USING DECORATIVE SCISSORS

Hold the scissors at least 2cm (^{3}/$_4$in) inside the edge of the card and cut a neat edge. Note that if you place it on the actual edge it tends to tear the card, not cut it.

EMBOSSING

1   Place the card on the stencil, right side down.
2   Using an embossing tool, gently press the card onto the stencil.
3   Turn the card over to reveal the embossed image.

RUBBER STAMPING

Holding an ink pad in your hand, gently dab ink all over your rubber stamp. Place the inked stamp gently on the card, pressing firmly with the flat of your hand or your fingers. Do not rock the stamp from side to side, as this will make the image uneven.

WET-TEARING MULBERRY PAPER

1   Using a clean paintbrush and water, draw the required shape.
2   Gently tear away the excess paper on one side.
3   Tear away the paper on the other sides.
4   Allow to dry, and then fluff the edges gently between finger and thumb.

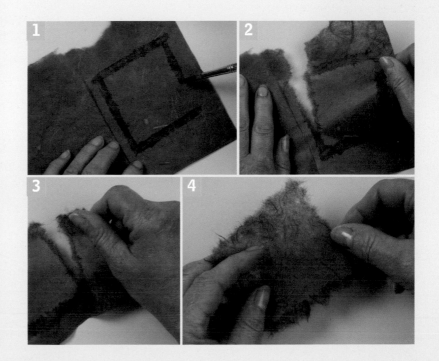

Working with wire and beads

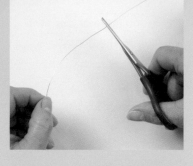

Cutting wire with scissors

There are lots of handy little tips I have picked up for working more easily and safely with wire and beads. Here are just a few:

Cutting wire with scissors
You do not need expensive pliers for these fine wires; an old pair of scissors is quite sufficient to snip them.

Using pointed tweezers
These are not essential, but they have many uses. Pointed tweezers help tremendously when you are grabbing wire or pushing the wire through, whereas fingers just get in the way.

Straightening wire between fingers
The copper wire is very soft and supple. To keep it running freely throughout your projects and to stop it knotting, run your finger and thumb frequently down its length.

Backstitching
This technique is just like backstitching in sewing. I use it to attach tiny beads firmly to the wire.

Picking up beads
It is easier to pick up small, fiddly beads if you moisten a finger (not too wet, or the beads will stick), dip it in the beads to pick a few up and thread them straight from your finger.

Using pointed tweezers

Straightening wire between fingers

Backstitching to attach beads to wire

Picking up beads

Winding spirals or coils of wire

Winding spirals of wire

To make spirals with your wire, use objects with a circular cross-section such as cocktail sticks or thin pencils. Wrap the wire round and round, pushing it together to create a coil or spiral, and ease gently off the stick. The smaller the diameter of the stick, the smaller your spiral will be.

Sprinkling on beads

If you need to use beads for decoration, use a small brush to place glue (PVA or PPA is adequate for this task) on the area you wish to decorate. Sprinkle the beads over the glued area, allow to dry, then gently tip off the excess.

Sprinkling on beads for decoration

Making a larger hole in a bead

When the holes in beads are too small, you may need to poke them though with the point of a sharp needle. I find the large pins with round heads are easier to work with.

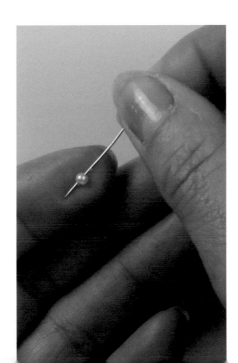

Making a larger hole

Working the beads

Before you make any of the projects, practise threading or knitting the beads. Spherical beads are perfect as they give an extremely even finish.

Use new packets of the same size beads. If they vary in size the finished product will be uneven. The first three projects use a heart as it is one of the easiest shapes to

make. Fairly large beads 28-gauge wire are best for beginners. Thread the beads on either side of the wire; you will soon establish a preference.

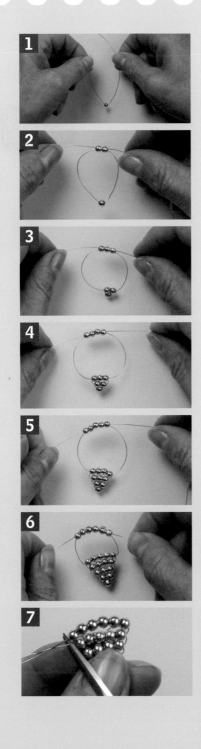

You will need
- 28-gauge gold wire
- 4mm gold beads

1. Cut 30cm (12in) of wire. Pass bead to centre. Bend wire to hold it in place.
2. Thread 2 beads on one side of wire about 2cm (1in) from end. Form a circle by passing the second wire through the 2 beads. Pull both wires evenly, until the beads sit on the first bead.
3. Thread and knit 3 beads.
4. Thread and knit 4 beads.
5. Thread and knit 5 beads.
6. Thread and knit 6 beads.
7. Pass ends of wire through last row to secure. Trim ends.
8. Cut 15cm (6in) of wire. Pass through 3 beads from either side of the last row.
9. Thread and knit 3 beads
10. Thread and knit 2 beads.
11. Secure ends by threading through the last row. Trim.
12. Add more wire and repeat step 9 for the other side.
13. Repeat step 10.
14. Repeat step 11 to complete the motif. Trim ends.

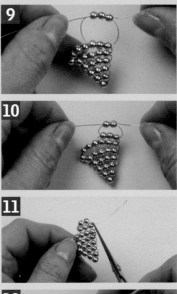

Adding more wire

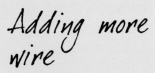

You may run out of wire part-way through a project, but it is easy to add more. Pass the ends of the original wire through the last row. Cut another length of wire and pass through the last row, ready to continue.

Crafty Touch

Keep the wires as straight as possible by passing continually between finger and thumb as you work. If they become bent and difficult to use, cut them off and join in more wire.

Safety tips

Knives and scissors

Make sure knives and scissors are sharp. Accidents can happen so, when cutting, bear the following rules in mind:

- use a firm, tidy surface
- take care when using a plastic ruler. It's better to use a metal safety ruler which will protect your fingers
- never cut on a wood surface, as the wood will grip the blade and make it hard to control
- when not in use, retract knife blades or replace blade covers
- keep sharp implements like scissors, needles and knives away from the edge of the work surface, preferably in a tray or box
- dispose of used blades carefully

Adhesives and colouring materials

Make sure you read and understand the manufacturer's recommendations on use and storage before working with adhesives and paints.

General

Make sure beads, wire or small metal parts are firmly attached, so your design does not fall apart. Never give cards with tiny decorations or beads to small children.

Adhesives

Glue sticks

These are a must for most gluing projects. They are easy and safe to use, and allow a little drying time to move projects around if needed.

Double-sided adhesive tape

This is good for most gluing projects in card-making, exceptionally good for glossy surfaces, but once stuck you cannot move them again.

Glue dots

These are great for sticking the beaded projects to your cards. They are non-messy and can be repositioned if needed.

Adhesive foam pads and dots

The foam pads give a 3D effect by raising the object or card up a little from the base card. They can be cut to size if necessary.

HEART OF GOLD

This card is ideal for a wedding anniversary, Valentine's Day
or just to tell someone special you love him – or her! Change the
colour of the heart or card to suit the person or the occasion.

Finished size
15 x 15cm (6 x 6in)

You will need...

Motif
- 28-gauge gold wire
- 31 x 4mm gold beads

Card
- White card 30 x 15cm (12 x 6in), folded
- Blue pearlized card 11 x 11cm (4¼ x 4¼ in)
- White card 10 x 10cm (4 x 4in)
- Gold vellum 9.5 x 9.5cm (3¾ x 3¾in)
- Gold webbing 8 x 8cm (3 x 3in)
- Spare piece of blue pearlized card
- Blue organza ribbon bow
- Gold thread
- Double-sided adhesive tape
- Glue dots
- Corner punch
- Gift tag punch

1 Assemble the card by gluing the small white square on to the blue square, then glue both of them to the base card.

2 Cut the corners of the vellum using the corner punch.

3 Wrap gold thread round the corners and secure at the back. Glue the vellum to the white card, and glue the gold webbing to the centre.

4 Cut the gift tag using a special punch, or cut your own shape with scissors. Punch a small hole in it using the hole punch.

5 Attach the heart using glue dots. Wrap the wire round the bow, then thread through the punched hole and attach using foam pads.

Crafty touch

At the end off a project, if the wire will not pass right through a row of threaded beads, just take it through one or two beads to secure it.

Threading instructions

To make the heart, follow steps 1–14 as for the example project (see page 16).

LOVE HEART

This card is really easy and quick to make, and the combination
of white and lilac always looks fresh and clean.

Finished size
15 x 10cm (6 x 4in)

You will need...

Motif
- 28-gauge silver wire
- 31 x 4mm glass beads

Card
- White textured card 30 x 15cm (12 x 6in), folded
- White mulberry paper, torn to 9 x 8cm (3½ x 3in)
- Small piece of white card
- Lilac skeleton leaf
- Narrow lilac ribbon
- 3 glass beads
- Glitter glue
- Glue stick or double-sided adhesive tape

1 Wet-tear the mulberry paper (p.13), and attach to the front of the white card.

2 Attach a skeleton leaf to the mulberry paper using glue stick.

3 Cut a length of lilac ribbon and thread on the beads.

4 Attach the ribbon to the inside of the card.

5 Glue the heart to a spare piece of white card. Trim round the edge, and then attach to the mulberry paper. Decorate with glitter glue.

Crafty touch

This card could also be used for Valentine's Day or a special anniversary.

Threading instructions

To make the heart, follow steps 1–14 as for the example project (see page 16).

VALENTINE HEARTS

These three little hearts are made in the same way
as the previous projects, but look completely
different because smaller beads are used.

Finished size
12.5 x 12.5cm (5 x 5in)

You will need...

Materials
- 34-gauge wire
- 31 red rocaille beads

Card
- Ready-made red aperture card 12.5 x 12.5cm (5 x 5in)
- Cream textured card 8.5 x 8.5cm (3½ x 3½in)
- Glue stick
- Glue dots
- Pearl dimensional paint

1 Insert the cream card and attach to the back of the red aperture card using the glue stick.

2 Attach the hearts using glue dots.

3 Decorate carefully with the pearl paint.

Crafty touch

Change the colours for a completely different look.

Threading instructions

To make the heart, follow steps 1–14 as for the example project (see page 16).

WEDDING CAKE

This beautiful vellum paper is perfect for a wedding card,
and the luscious organza ribbon finishes it off beautifully.

Finished size
15 x 15cm (6 x 6in)

You will need...

Motif
- 64 pearl beads
- 32 silver beads

Card
- 34- or 28-gauge silver wire
- White card 30 x 15cm (12 x 6in), folded
- Vellum paper 16 x 15cm (6½ x 6in)
- Pink pearlized card 5 x 4cm (2 x 1½in)
- White webbing/angel hair 7 x 6cm (3 x 2½in)
- Pink organza ribbon
- Glue stick or double-sided adhesive tape
- Glue dots
- Fancy craft scissors with deckle edge

1 Cut and trim the vellum with fancy craft scissors.

2 Fold the left edge of the vellum and attach to the back of the card, on the fold.

3 Take the organza ribbon round the front of the card and tie in a bow.

4 Trim the pink card using fancy craft scissors. Cover with the webbing and glue the edges to the back. Attach to the front of the vellum.

5 Attach the motif using glue dots.

Crafty touch

You may have to enlarge the hole in the pearl beads before use – see page 15.

Threading instructions

1 Cut 45cm (18 in) of wire. Thread 11 pearl beads but do not knit them.

2 Next 11 rows: Thread and knit 11 silver beads; 11 pearl beads; 9 pearl beads; 9 silver beads; 9 pearl beads; 7 pearl beads; 7 silver beads; 7 pearl beads; 5 pearl beads; 5 silver beads; 5 pearl beads.

3 Pass wires through. Trim.

HAPPY BIRTHDAY

These pink glass beads look just like icing, so the only sensible thing
to do is to use them to make a cake!

Finished size
15 x 15cm (6 x 6in)

You will need...

Motif
- 60 pink beads
- 34- or 28-gauge silver wire
- 4 pink bugle beads
- 4 yellow embroidery beads

Card
- Pink card 30 x 15cm
  (12 x 6in), folded
- Green perforated card
  15 x 11.5cm (6 x 4½in)
- Patterned paper 15 x 7.5cm
  (6 x 3in)
- Pink gingham paper
  6 x 6cm (2¼ x 2¼in)
- Pink gingham ribbon
- Glue stick or double-sided
  adhesive tape
- Foam dots
- Glue dots
- Fancy craft scissors

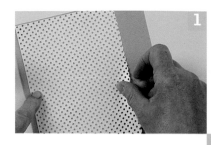

1 Attach the green
perforated card
to the front of the pink card
using the glue stick or
double-sided tape.

2 Attach the patterned paper
to the green card.

3 Attach the gingham
square using foam dots.

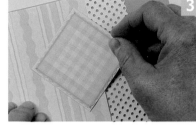

4 Attach the cake motif
using glue dots.

5 Attach the bow
using a glue dot.

Crafty touch

The beads also come in pale
blue, white and green, so you
can vary the colour to suit the
recipient.

Threading instructions

1 Cut 30cm (12in) of wire.
Thread and knit 6 rows of 10
beads. Fasten off ends.
2 Cut 15cm (6in) of wire. Pass
through 2 beads at one end
of top row. Pass back up
between beads 2 and 3.
3 Thread 1 bugle and 1 yellow
bead. Take wire over yellow

bead and pass through
bugle bead again. Pass back
up between beads 2 and 3.
Pass through 2 more beads.
Pass back up between beads
4 and 5.
4 Repeat step 3 to end of row.
Fasten off and trim wires.

CRYSTAL BAG

This pretty handbag is fun to make in glass beads, which come in a wide range of pretty colours. Why not make one for a special **girlfriend's** birthday?

Finished size

15 x 15cm (6 x 6in)

You will need...

Motif

- 28- or 34-gauge gold or silver wire
- 31 glass beads
- 36 embroidery beads
- 1 silver bead

Card

- White card 30 x 15cm (12 x 6in), folded
- Green backing paper 7 x 7cm ($2^3/_4$ x $2^3/_4$in) x 4
- White hand-made paper 9 x 9cm ($3^1/_2$ x $3^1/_2$in)
- Green pearlized card 4.5 x 4.5cm (2 x 2in)
- White card 4 x 4cm ($1^1/_2$ x $1^1/_2$in)
- Feather
- Glue stick or double-sided adhesive tape
- Glue dots
- Double-sided adhesive foam pads
- Fancy craft scissors with deckle edge

Crafty touch

When you work with larger beads, it does not matter which wire you use. It is perhaps easier to work with 28-gauge, but it looks daintier with 34-gauge.

1 Attach the squares of green backing paper to the front of the white card.

2 Trim the hand-made paper using the craft scissors and attach using foam pads for a raised effect.

3 Attach the small square of green pearlized card using foam pads.

4 Trim the small square of white card using the craft scissors. Attach to the centre of the green square.

5 Attach the motif using a glue dot, then attach the feather by pressing the end into the same glue dot.

Threading instructions

1 Cut 30cm (12 in) of wire. Thread 9 beads to the centre and bend the ends.
2 Thread and knit 7 beads.
3 Thread and knit 6 beads.
4 Thread and knit 5 beads.
5 Thread 2 clear, 1 silver and 2 clear beads, and knit.
6 Thread about 38 silver embroidery beads on the longest wire. Pass the end through the last row of beads to form a handle. Trim ends.
7 Secure the second wire by passing back through the last row.

PINK BAG

This motif is a little more difficult because of the size of the beads
and the number of beads in a row. You will need patience
and good eyesight – or your glasses!

Finished size

10 x 10cm (4 x 4in)

You will need...

Motif

- 34-gauge silver or gold wire
- 81 pink embroidery beads
- 24 silver embroidery beads

Card

- Pink card 20 x 10cm (8 x 4in), folded
- Deeper pink card 10 x 5cm (4 x 2in)
- Pearlized card 9 x 7cm (3¹/₂ x 2¹/₂in)
- Purple webbing ribbon
- Feather
- Glue dots
- Glue stick
- Double-sided adhesive tape
- 5cm (2in) circle punch

1 Attach the deeper pink card to the front of the pink card.

2 Punch a hole in the centre of the pearlized card.

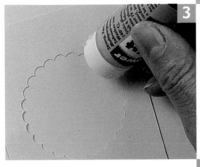

3 Attach the webbing ribbon to the back of the hole using a glue stick.

4 Attach the pearlized card to the main card with foam pads, then attach the motif using a glue dot. Tuck the end of the feather into the same glue dot to attach.

Crafty touch

If, when using the glue stick, you find that the webbing comes unstuck, use double-sided tape.

Threading instructions

1 Cut 30cm (12in) of wire and pass 16 pink beads into the centre.

2 Thread and knit 14 beads.

3 Thread and knit 13 beads.

4 Thread and knit 11 beads.

5 Thread and knit 10 beads.

6 Thread and knit 9 beads.

7 Thread 4 pink, 1 silver and 4 pink beads, and knit.

8 Using the longer wire, thread 23 silver beads. Pass the end of the wire back through the last row of beads to form a handle. Pass through several beads in the next row down to secure.

9 Pass the other end of the wire through the last row to secure. Trim ends.

GLASS BASKET

Baskets are such a useful centrepiece for cards, and they can be adorned with a variety of flowers. These beige glass beads came from an old necklace, and are the perfect colour for a basket.

Finished size
15 x 15cm (6 x 6in)

You will need...

Motif
- 30 glass beads
- 40 mixed embroidery beads
- 28-gauge copper wire

Card
- White card 30 x 15cm (12 x 6in), folded
- Orange mulberry paper 14 x 14cm (5½ x 5½in), wet-torn
- Black mulberry paper 12.5 x 12.5cm (5 x 5in), wet-torn
- Leafy paper 10 x 10cm (4 x 4in)
- White hand-made paper 10 x 10cm (4 x 4in)
- White card
- Orange card
- Green mulberry paper
- Ribbon
- Yellow accent beads
- Spare 28-gauge silver wire
- Glue stick or double-sided adhesive tape
- Glue dot
- Adhesive foam pads
- Fancy craft scissors
- Tiny daisy punch

1 Cut a large circle in the centre of the square of leafy paper. Decorate with glitter glue and allow to dry.

2 Attach the hand-made paper to the hole using foam pads for a relief effect.

3 Layer the black and the orange mulberry paper on the base card. Punch out orange and white daisies from spare card.

4 Cut four oblongs of green mulberry paper about 2cm (1in) long. Glue them together with wire between. Trim to a leaf shape with fancy scissors.

5 Attach wire to the back of each flower. Decorate with accent beads. Fix basket, bow, leaves and flowers in place using glue dots.

Crafty touch

Accent beads are tiny beads without holes. Apply glue to the area to be decorated, then sprinkle on the beads. Shake off the excess and leave to dry for a few hours.

Threading instructions

1 Cut 30cm (12 in) of wire and thread 4 beads.
2 Thread and knit 5 beads.
3 Thread and knit 6 beads.
4 Thread and knit 7 beads.
5 Thread and knit 8 beads.

6 Thread about 40 small beads on the longest wire (handle).
7 Pass end of the wire through the last row of beads.
8 Secure the wires by passing through the last row.

PEARLY BASKET

The pearl beads give this basket a different look. It has a rounded shape,
and is made in a slightly different way from the previous project.

Finished size

15 x 15cm (6 x 6in)

You will need...

Motif

- 65 white pearl beads
- 50 glass embroidery beads
- 28-gauge silver wire

Card

- White card 30 x 15cm (12 x 6in), folded
- White card 14 x 14cm (5^1/$_2$ x 5^1/$_2$in)
- Yellow mulberry paper 10 x 10cm (4 x 4in)
- Blue pearlized card 8 x 8cm (3 x 3in)
- White card 7 x 7cm (2^1/$_2$ x 2^1/$_2$in)
- Blue pearlized card 5 x 5cm
- Bow
- Yellow dimensional paint
- Glue stick or double-sided adhesive tape
- Glue dots
- Flowers
- Flower stamp
- Yellow ink pad
- 5cm (2in) square scalloped punch/fancy craft scissors

Crafty touch

Once you have made one or two baskets you will be able to make any size and shape that you want.

1 Stamp a flower design in yellow on the largest piece of white card.

2 Layer and attach the mulberry paper, larger blue card, smaller white card and the smaller blue card, trimmed with the punch.

3 Attach the basket using glue dots, then attach the bow to the handle.

4 Slide the ends of the flowers into the glue dots to secure.

5 Decorate card with dimensional paint.

Threading instructions

1 Cut 45cm (18in) of wire and thread 4 beads.

2 Thread and knit 5 beads, then add 1 bead to each end of the wire.

3 Thread and knit 8 beads, then add 1 bead to the end of each row (10 beads).

4 Thread and knit 11 beads.

5 Thread and knit 11 beads. Repeat three times.

6 Using the longer wire, thread 50 glass embroidery beads.

7 Rethread end of handle through last row of basket, then through the next row down to secure. Trim ends.

8 Secure other end.

ORANGE BASKET

This versatile card is ideal for many occasions, and seed beads
are used for this version. The beads vary in size and shape which gives
a slightly irregular appearance.

Finished size
15 x 15cm (6 x 6in)

You will need...

Motif
- 60 orange seed beads
- 60 (colour) embroidery beads
- 28-gauge wire

Making the card
- Cream card 30 x 15cm (12 x 6in), folded
- Striped background paper 14 x 14cm (5¹/₂ x 5¹/₂in)
- Cream pearlized card 11 x 11cm (4¹/₂ x 4¹/₂in)
- Green dotted paper 10 x 10cm (4 x 4in)
- Cream pearlized card 5.5 x 5.5cm (2¹/₄ x 2¹/₄in)
- Scraps of coloured paper
- Scraps of thin wire
- 6 small black beads
- Dried fern
- Bow
- Glue dots
- Glue stick or double-sided adhesive tape
- Fancy craft scissors with scalloped edge

1 Trim the cream pearlized card squares using craft scissors. Layer and attach the various cards and papers to the front of the base card.

2 Punch out 12 flower shapes. Thread a bead on a piece of wire, twist ends to form stem.

3 Pierce hole through centre of flower with a pin, and pass a short length of wire through the hole. Repeat to make 6 flowers.

4 Glue the dried greenery and basket to the card using glue dots.

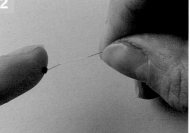

5 Arrange the flowers in basket and push the wires into the glue dot to attach. Attach the bow using a glue dot.

Crafty touch
Change the colour of the beads used for the basket or the handle for a completely different look.

Threading instructions
1 Cut 30cm (12in) of wire and thread 5 beads.
2 Thread and knit 7 beads.
3 Thread and knit 9 beads.
4 Thread and knit 11 beads.
5 Thread and knit 13 beads.
6 Thread and knit 15 beads.
7 Thread up to 60 embroidery beads on the longer wire. Pass end through last row.
8 Secure ends by threading through the last row again.

GOLDEN TREE

This motif is quick and easy to make, and the coloured beads
are placed at random. Use any size beads, but the smaller the beads,
the more you will need for each row.

Finished size
15 x 15cm (6 x 6in)

You will need...

Motif
- 26 gold beads
- 4 red beads
- 9 random-coloured beads
- 1 large bead
- 28-gauge wire

Card
- Red card 12 x 6in (30 x 15cm), folded
- White card with seasonal pattern 13.5 x 13.5cm (5½ x 5½in)
- Red mulberry paper 11.5 x 11.5cm (4½ x 4½in), wet-torn
- White card 10 x 10cm (4 x 4in)
- Scraps of blue and green mulberry paper
- Snow netting
- Star
- Glue stick or double-sided adhesive tape
- Glue dot

1 Assemble the patterned card and the red mulberry paper.

2 Wet-tear blue and green mulberry paper to form hill and sky shapes. Attach to the white card.

3 Cover the picture with the netting and glue the edges to the back of the card. Attach to the front of the card with double-sided tape.

4 Attach the tree and the star using glue dots.

Crafty touch

Attach a pin to a tree motif to make an attractive brooch to wear over the festive period.

Threading instructions

1 Cut 35cm (14in) of wire. Thread 2 red beads.
2 Thread and knit 2 red beads.
3 Thread and knit 2 red beads.
4 Thread 3 beads on each wire but do not knit. Bend ends of wire to keep beads in place (8 beads on wire).
5 Thread and knit 7 beads.
6 Thread and knit 6 beads.
7 Thread and knit 5 beads.
8 Thread and knit 4 beads.
9 Thread and knit 3 beads.
10 Thread and knit 2 beads.
11 Thread and knit 1 bead.
12 Secure ends by passing through the last row.

GREEN TREE

This motif made from seed beads looks very different from the tree made with round beads. The oval shape and varied sizes of the beads produce a more textured tree, and you will need more beads to complete the project.

Finished size
15 x 10cm (6 x 4in)

You will need...

Motif
- 70 green seed beads
- 9 red seed beads
- 4 red round beads
- 3 gold round beads
- 28-gauge wire

Card
- White card 15 x 10cm (6 x 4in), folded
- Green card 14.5 x 9.5cm ($5^1/_2$ x $3^3/_4$in)
- White card 9 x 7.5cm ($3^1/_2$ x 3 in)
- Gold card 7 x 5.5cm ($2^3/_4$ x $2^1/_4$in)
- Red webbing
- Fancy craft scissors with deckle edges
- Glue stick or double-sided adhesive tape
- Foam pads
- Glue dots
- Glitter glue

1 Trim the edges of the white and gold cards using fancy scissors. Emboss a square frame just inside the edge of the white card.

2 Attach the red webbing to the back of the gold card, using double-sided tape top and bottom.

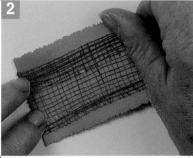

3 Attach the gold card on to the embossed square, using foam pads.

4 Attach the tree using glue dots and decorate the card with glitter glue.

Crafty touch

Thread the round bauble beads at random throughout the motif.

Threading instructions

1 Cut 40cm (14in) of wire and thread 2 red beads.
2 Thread and knit 3 red beads.
3 Thread and knit 4 red beads.
4 Thread and knit 4 green beads. Add 4 green beads to each wire without knitting.
5 Thread and knit 11 beads.
6 Thread and knit 10 beads.
7 Thread and knit 9 beads.
8 Thread and knit 8 beads.
9 Thread and knit 7 beads.
10 Thread and knit 6 beads.
11 Thread and knit 5 beads.
12 Thread and knit 4 beads.
13 Thread and knit 3 beads.
14 Thread and knit 2 beads.
15 Thread and knit 1 bead.
16 Secure ends by rethreading through last row.

PINK BELL

Bells are a traditional motif for Christmas cards, and you can change
the colour of the beads for a different effect. This motif can also
be made from tiny embroidery beads or pretty glass beads.

Finished size
18 x 10cm (7 x 4in)

You will need...

Motif
- 32 round pearl beads
- 9 round silver beads
- 1 large silver bead
- 28-gauge wire

Card
- White card 18 x 20cm (7 x 8in), folded
- Silver card 16.5 x 9cm (6$\frac{1}{2}$ x 3$\frac{1}{2}$in)
- Pink card 15 x 7.5cm (6 x 3in)
- Pink card 6.5 x 4.5cm (2$\frac{1}{2}$ x 1$\frac{3}{4}$in)
- White card 6 x 4cm (2$\frac{1}{2}$ x 1$\frac{1}{2}$in)
- White-flecked fine paper 18 x 10cm (7 x 4in)
- Pink ribbon
- Glue stick or double-sided adhesive tape
- Glue dots

1 Attach the small rectangle of white card to the small rectangle of pink card.

2 Layer the white-flecked paper on the pink card, then attach to the base card. Attach the rectangle of pink and white card.

3 Attach the bell to the centre of the card using a glue dot.

4 Tie a bow to the top of the bell.

Crafty touch

Change the colour of the beads and card, and use the same motif for a wedding card.

Threading instructions

1 Cut 30cm (12in) of wire and thread on large silver bead.
2 Thread and knit 2 pearl beads.
3 Thread 4 beads on each wire (10 beads) but do not knit. Bend wire at each end.
4 Thread and knit 9 silver beads.
5 Thread and knit 8 pearl beads.
6 Thread and knit 7 pearl beads.
7 Thread and knit 6 pearl beads.
8 Thread and knit 5 silver beads.
9 Thread and knit 4 silver beads.
10 Pass the longer end of wire through the last row again leaving a loop.
11 Secure the other end by passing through the last row.

43

PURPLE BELL

It is fun to use purple for Christmas instead of the usual red and green.
The embossed border adds an extra dimension

44

Finished size
15 x 15cm (6 x 6in)

You will need...

Motif
- 1 large silver bead
- 9 purple beads
- 40 silver beads
- 14 purple embroidery beads

Card
- Purple card 30 x 15cm (12 x 6in), folded
- White card 14 x 14cm (5$\frac{1}{2}$ x 5$\frac{1}{2}$in)
- Purple card 10.5 x 10.5cm (4$\frac{1}{4}$ x 4$\frac{1}{4}$in)
- Silver card 10 x 10cm (4 x 4in)
- White card 9.5 x 9.5cm (3$\frac{3}{4}$ x 3$\frac{3}{4}$in)
- Purple ribbon
- Small purple bow
- Glue stick or double-sided adhesive tape
- Glue dots
- Glitter glue
- Purple dimensional paint

1 Dry emboss a frame 11.5 x 11.5cm (4$\frac{1}{2}$ x 4$\frac{1}{2}$in) on the larger piece of white card. Layer the cards as shown and attach to the base card.

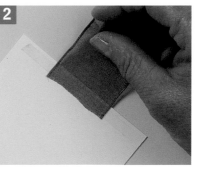

2 Attach ribbon by gluing the ends to the centre back of the white card.

3 Attach the ribbon-trimmed card to the centre of the base card.

4 Attach the bell to the ribbon using glue dots. Decorate the card with glitter glue and paint.

Crafty touch

This card was made for Christmas, but would be equally suitable for an anniversary card.

Threading instructions

Thread and knit the beads in exactly the same way as for the previous project, but using embroidery beads for the handle instead of just the plain wire.

YULE CROWN

This traditional Christmas crown can be made with lots of different beads but I like these shiny round ones that come in gold, silver, pink, purple and blue. The card is finished with a ribbon threaded with gold beads.

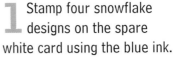

Finished size
12.5 x 12.5cm (5 x 5in)

You will need...

Motif
- 39 gold beads
- 3 large blue beads
- 28-gauge gold wire

Card
- White card 25 x 12.5cm (10 x 5in), folded
- Blue holographic card 9 x 9cm (3½ x 3½ in)
- White card 8 x 8cm (3 x 3in)
- White card 5 x 5cm (2 x 2in)
- Blue holographic card 4 x 4cm (1½ x 1½in)
- White card 3 x 3cm (1¼ x 1¼in)
- Small piece of white card
- Snowflake rubber stamp
- Blue ink pad
- Thin blue ribbon
- 2 gold beads
- Double-sided adhesive tape
- Glue stick
- Glitter glue
- Square punch

Crafty touch

When attaching card to holographic card, remember to use double-sided tape.

1 Stamp four snowflake designs on the spare white card using the blue ink.

2 Punch/cut out the squares and glue to the 8 x 8cm (3 x 3in) white card. Glue to the large holographic card.

3 Layer the smaller piece of holographic card on to the medium-size card and glue to the centre of the snowflake design.

4 Cover the smaller white card with glitter glue, then allow to dry.

5 Fix the glittery square to the centre of the card. Attach the crown using glue dots. Add two beads to the ribbon and attach to the inside front of the card.

Threading instructions

1 Cut 25cm (10in) of wire and thread 6 beads.
2 Thread and knit 7 beads.
3 Thread and knit 8 beads.
4 Thread and knit 9 beads. Secure ends.
5 Cut 15cm (6in) of wire. Pass through centre 3 beads.
6 Thread and knit 2 beads.
7 Thread and knit 1 bead.
8 Thread and knit 1 larger bead. Secure ends.
9 Add 15cm (6in) of wire through either right or left 3 beads.
10 Thread and knit 2 beads.
11 Thread and knit 1 bead.
12 Thread and knit 1 larger bead. Secure ends.
13 Repeat steps 9–12 on final 3 beads.

CROWN, BELL AND TREE

I love anything in miniature, and the motifs from the three previous projects, worked in tiny embroidery beads, look fantastic all on one card.

Finished size
21 x 10cm (8 x 4in)

You will need...

Motifs
* Embroidery beads –
  quantities as for the three
  previous projects.

Card
* White card 21 x 21cm
  (8 x 8in), folded
* Gold card 12 x 6cm
  (4³/₄ x 2¹/₄in)
* Small piece of white card
* Christmas ribbon
* Glue stick or double-sided
  adhesive tape
* Glue dots
* Square 'postage stamp'
  punch
* Corner punch

1 Place the ribbon over
the front of the card.
Attach the ends to the inside
using double-sided tape.

2 Punch squares in gold card
using the square punch,
then punch the corners.

3 Cut spare white card
just smaller than the
piece of gold card, and glue
it underneath.

4 Glue the white card
to the ribbon.

5 Attach the motifs using
glue dots.

Crafty touch

Make two tiny matching
motifs and attach them to
earring findings.

Threading instructions

Make each of the motifs as in the previous three projects,
substituting tiny embroidery beads for the beads listed.

PINK GLASS VASE

This pretty vase of glass beads says anything from Best Wishes
to Happy Mother's Day or Happy Birthday. The vibrant hand-made paper
is also used for the flowers.

Finished size

15 x 15cm (6 x 6in)

You will need...

Motif

- 74 pink glass beads
- 28-gauge red wire

Card

- White card 30 x 15cm (12 x 6in), folded
- Multi-coloured hand-made paper 13.5 x 13.5cm (5 x 5in)
- Green wire
- 3 yellow beads
- Pink paper-covered wire
- Pink raffia
- Glue stick or double-sided adhesive tape
- Glue dots
- Flower punch
- Cocktail stick

1 Tie the paper wire into a circular frame. Assemble the paper, making sure there is a dark section in the centre.

2 Cut and assemble the flowers by threading green wire through the centre of the punched shapes.

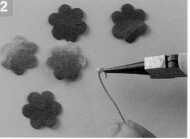

3 Wind the wire coils round the cocktail stick.

4 Assemble the vase and fix double-sided tape on the back.

5 Turn over and secure to front of card, adding a glue dot under each flower head. Finish with a raffia bow.

Crafty touch

For a different look, vary the paper background and arrange craft flowers in the vase – there are so many available.

Threading instructions

1 Thread 5 beads.
2 Thread and knit 7 beads.
3 Thread and knit 9 beads.
4 Thread and knit 11 beads.
5 Thread and knit 10 beads.
6 Thread and knit 9 beads.
7 Thread and knit 8 beads.
8 Thread and knit 6 beads.
9 Thread and knit 4 beads.
10 Thread and knit 5 beads.
11 Thread and knit 6 beads. Secure ends.

DAISY, DAISY

Many different shapes of vase can be achieved by varying
the previous project slightly.

Finished size

15 x 10cm (6 x 4in)

You will need...

Motif

- 82 green glass beads
- 28-gauge green wire

Card

- Green card 21 x 15cm
  (8 x 6in), folded
- Very pale green card
  14 x 9.5cm (5 x 3³/₄in)
- Spare green beads
- Green webbing/ angel hair
- Foam dots
- Glue stick or double-sided
  adhesive tape
- Glue dot
- Daisy punch

1 Cut a square aperture in the front of the green card. Attach the webbing to the back of the aperture in the card using double-sided tape.

2 Cut a square the same size from the pale green card. Carefully cut away another 2mm all round. Attach the card to the base card.

3 Punch daisies from pale green card and glue a tiny bead carefully to the centre of each.

4 Take the 2mm 'frame' that was cut away in step 2, and attach it diagonally to the aperture as shown.

5 Attach the vase and flowers using tiny pieces cut from foam dots to give a 3D effect.

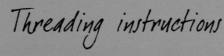

Crafty touch

This card also looks stunning made in black and white.

Threading instructions

1 Thread 5 beads.
2 Thread and knit 6 beads.
3 Thread and knit 7 beads
4 Thread and knit 8 beads.
5 Thread and knit 9 beads.
6 Thread and knit 10 beads.
7 Thread and knit 9 beads.
8 Thread and knit 8 beads.
9 Thread and knit 7 beads.
10 Thread and knit 6 beads.
11 Thread and knit 7 beads.
    Secure ends.

BABY LOVE

This tiny pram is made from pearl embroidery beads with black beads for the wheels. It is perfect for a new baby, and not too difficult to make.

Finished size

15 x 15cm (6 x 6in)

You will need...

Motif

- 54 pearl embroidery beads
- 21 black embroidery beads
- 7 silver embroidery beads
- 34-gauge silver wire

Card

- White card 30 x 15cm
  (12 x 6in), folded
- Purple checked backing
  paper 12.5 x 12.5cm
  (5 x 5in)
- White card 10.5 x 10.5cm
  (4³/₄ x 4³/₄in)
- Purple dotted paper
  10 x 10cm (4 x 4in)
- Silver pearlized
  pre-embossed card 9 x 9cm
  (3 x 3in)
- Purple pearlized card
  4 x 3.5cm (1³/₄ x 1¹/₂in)
- Silver pearlized card
  3 x 2.5cm (1¹/₄ x 1in)
- Spare purple pearlised card
- Purple dimensional paint
- Glue stick or double-sided
  adhesive tape
- Glue dots
- 'Postage stamp' punch
  or fancy craft scissors

Crafty touch

Make the pram motifs
in neutral colours, then use
on a card of the appropriate
colour.

1 Assemble the cards
and paper.

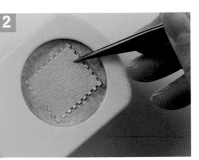

2 Punch the smallest card
using a postage stamp
punch, or trim using craft
scissors.

3 Attach to the centre
of the card.

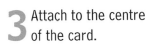

4 Decorate with dimensional
paint before adding the
motif using a glue dot.

Threading instructions

1 Thread 7 beads.

2 Thread and knit 8 beads.

3 Thread and knit 9 beads.

4 Thread and knit 10 beads.

5 Using the longer wire, thread
7 silver, then 1 black bead.
Leave wire.

6 Take the other wire over black
bead and through 7 silver
beads. Pass through 4 beads
in previous row. Pull up.

7 Using the same wire plus the
wire left in step 5, thread and
knit 6 beads for the hood.

8 Thread and knit 6 beads.

9 Thread and knit 5 beads.
Secure ends.

10 Cut 15cm (6in) of wire. Pass
through bottom row. Add 10
black beads to each end.

11 Pass one end of wire through
first two beads to form circle.

12 Repeat to form second wheel.
Secure ends.

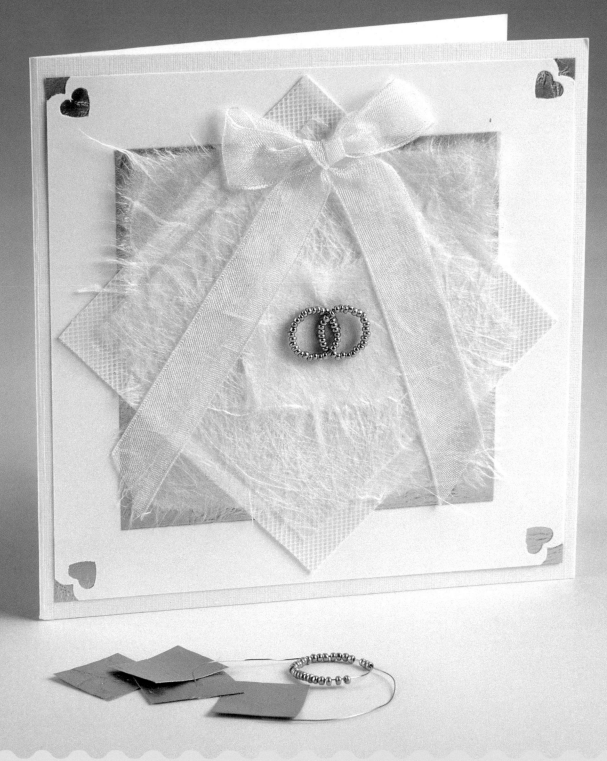

TWO GOLD RINGS

Layering in lots of materials complements the simple beading.
The beautiful organza ribbon is available in many sumptuous shades.

Finished size

15 x 15cm (6 x 6in)

You will need...

Motif
* Gold beads – about 30 for each ring
* 28-gauge gold wire

Card
* White card 30 x 15cm (12 x 6in), folded
* White card 14 x 14cm ($5^1/_2$ x $5^1/_2$in)
* Gold card 10 x 10cm (4 x 4in)
* White mulberry paper 10 x 10cm (4 x 4in)
* White pearlized card 10 x 10cm (4 x 4in)
* Mulberry paper 4 x 4cm (2 x 2in), torn
* Gold card 2 x 2cm ($^3/_4$ x $^3/_4$in) x 4
* White netting 10 x 10cm (4 x 4in)
* Webbing ribbon/angel hair 8cm (3in)
* White organza ribbon
* Glue stick or double-sided adhesive tape
* Glue dot
* Heart corner punch

1 Trim the white card using the corner heart punch.

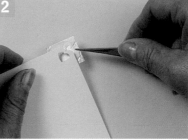

2 Glue the tiny sqaures of gold card under the corners.

3 Assemble all the cards and glue in place. Attach the piece of mulberry paper.

4 Attach the pearlized card, the white netting and the webbing ribbon/angel hair, all on the diagonal.

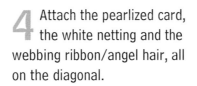

5 Attach the tiny square of mulberry paper. Attach the rings and the bow using glue dots.

Crafty touch

This card could be used for a wedding, anniversary or even an engagement card.

Threading instructions

1 Cut 5cm (2in) of wire and thread 30 beads.
2 Pass each end of the wire through 4–5 beads in opposite directions, then pull to secure.
3 Cut another length of wire and pass through the first circle of beads to join the rings together, then work the second ring in the same way.

NEW HOUSE

This lovely welcome to a new home is really quick to make.
Card and paper in a range of textures adds dimension.

Finished size
15 x 15cm (6 x 6in)

You will need...

Motif

- 34 round silver beads
- 18 round red beads
- 10 round blue beads
- 4 purple beads
- 28-gauge wire

Card

- White card 30 x 15cm (12 x 6in), folded
- Blue mulberry paper 13 x 13cm (5 x 5in)
- Silver punched card 11 x 11cm (4¼ x 4¼in)
- Multi-coloured corrugated card 9.5 x 9.5cm (3 x 3in)
- Silver punched card 5 x 5cm (2 x 2in)
- Glue stick or double-sided adhesive tape
- Glue dots

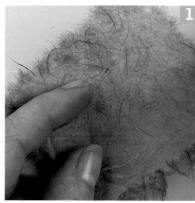

1 Wet-tear and glue mulberry paper to the front of the base card.

2 Layer and attach the larger piece of silver card, the corrugated card and the smaller silver card.

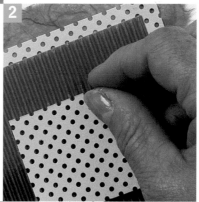

3 Attach the motif using glue dots.

Crafty touch

This motif works equally well made with really small beads to use on a tiny card.

Threading instructions

1. Thread 3 silver, 2 blue and 3 silver beads. Do not knit.
2. Thread and knit 3 silver, 2 blue and 3 silver beads (8 beads).
3. Thread and knit 1 silver, 1 purple, 1 silver, 2 blue, 1 silver, 1 purple, 1 silver bead (8 beads)
4. Repeat row 3.
5. Repeat row 2.
6. Thread and knit 8 silver beads.
7. Thread and knit 8 red beads.
8. Thread and knit 7 red beads.
9. Thread and knit 6 red beads. Secure ends.

CONGRATULATIONS

This project is is ideal for a party invitation or a special event.
It is simple to make, and glass beads add a realistic touch.

Finished size

15 x 15cm (6 x 6in)

You will need...

Bottle motif

- 106 burgundy glass embroidery beads
- 25 white embroidery beads
- 1 large silver bead
- 34-gauge wire

Glass motif

- 30 gold glass beads
- 34-gauge wire

Card

- Wine card 30 x 15cm (12 x 6in), folded
- Printed wine-coloured backing paper 14 x 14cm (5$\frac{1}{2}$ x 5$\frac{1}{2}$in)
- Wine mulberry paper 7.5 x 7.5cm (3 x 3in)
- Corrugated card 6 x 6cm (2$\frac{1}{2}$ x 2$\frac{1}{2}$in)
- Gemstones
- Glue stick or double-sided adhesive tape
- Glue dots
- Corner punch

Crafty Touch

Change the bottle colour and shape to represent a different drink.

1 Punch the corners of the card.

2 Assemble and attach the cards and paper.

3 Attach the motifs to the front of the card.

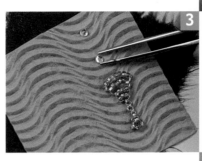

4 Decorate with gemstones to represent bubbles.

Threading instructions

Bottle

1 Thread 9 beads. Do not knit.
2 Thread and knit 9 beads.
3 Repeat row 2 three times.
4 Thread and knit 2 burgundy, 5 white and 2 burgundy beads.
5 Repeat row 6 five times.
6 Thread and knit 7 beads.
7 Thread and knit 5 beads.
8 Thread and knit 3 beads.
9 Repeat row 8 three times

10 Thread and knit large silver bead. Secure ends.

Glass

1 Thread 3 beads. Do not knit.
2 Thread and knit 2 beads.
3 Thread and knit 1 bead. Repeat four times.
4 Thread and knit 3 beads.
5 Thread and knit 4 beads.
6 Thread and knit 6 beads.
7 Thread and knit 8 beads. Secure ends.

61

PINK BUTTERFLY

Butterflies are popular with all ages, so this is an excellent
general-purpose card.

Finished size
15 x 15cm (6 x 6in)

You will need...

Motif
- 87 pink embroidery beads
- Gold 34-gauge wire

Card
- White card 30 x 15cm
  (12 x 6in), folded
- Pink gingham paper
  11 x 11cm (4$\frac{1}{2}$ x 4$\frac{1}{2}$in)
- White corrugated card
  10 x 10cm (4 x 4in)
- Pink card 7.5 x 7.5cm
  (3 x 3in)
- Pink card 7 x 7cm
  (2$\frac{3}{4}$ x 2$\frac{3}{4}$in)
- Flower ribbon
- Glitter glue
- Glue stick or double-sided
  adhesive tape
- Adhesive foam tape
- Square punch
- White ink-pad
- Netting pattern rubber
  stamp
- Very small flower punch

Crafty touch

Embroidery beads make
really dainty insects, but
children could make these
motifs using larger beads.

1 Layer and attach the gingham paper and the corrugated card.

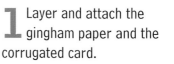

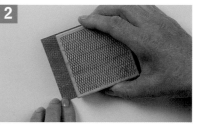

2 Stamp the larger pink card using white ink. Attach the smaller pink card for a 'frame' effect. Punch an aperture.

3 Attach the flower ribbon to the back of the aperture in the pink card.

4 Attach the pink frame using foam tape.

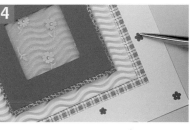

5 Punch out and attach the tiny flowers. Dot the centre of each with glitter glue. Attach the butterfly.

Threading instructions

Body
1 Pass 1 bead to centre of wire
2 Thread and knit 1 bead, seven times. Leave about 1cm ($\frac{1}{2}$in) of wire for antennae.

Upper wings
1 Cut 15cm (6in) wire and pass through fourth bead from top.
2 Thread 20 beads on one side. Pass through third bead.
3 Thread 20 beads on other side. Pass through third bead.

4 Twist ends together at the back to secure. Trim.

Lower wings
5 Cut 15cm (6in) of wire. Pass through fifth bead.
6 Thread 19 beads on one side. Pass through the fourth or fifth bead.
7 Thread 19 beads on second side. Complete wing.
8 Twist excess wire together at back, or leave to form legs.

63

SMALL DRAGONFLY

This simple card for all ages looks clean and fresh.
The motif is just 2cm (^{3}/4in) across.

Finished size

15 x 15cm (6 x 6in)

You will need...

Motif

- 41 pink embroidery beads
- 20 blue embroidery beads
- 1 larger blue bead
- 34-gauge wire

Card

- White card 30 x 15cm (12 x 6in), folded
- Blue patterned backing paper 11 x 11cm ($4^1/_2$ x $4^1/_2$in)
- White card 10 x 10cm (4 x 4in) x 2
- Blue rainbow ink pad
- Green ink pad
- Black ink pad
- Flower stamp
- Yellow dimensional paint
- Green dimensional paint
- Glue stick or double-sided adhesive tape
- Glue dots
- Small flower punch

1 Colour one of the squares of white card using the blue rainbow ink-pad by pressing gently over and over the card in the same place.

2 Use the green ink-pad just at the bottom. Stamp a flower design on the card using black ink.

3 Punch 7 tiny flowers and glue to centre of stamped flowers. Trim stamped card to 9 x 9cm ($3^1/_2$ x $3^1/_2$in).

4 Assemble the patterned paper and white card on the base card. Decorate the card and the flower centres using dimensional paint.

5 Attach the dragonfly using a glue dot.

Crafty Touch

If the wire will not pass through a bead again, use the bead below.

Threading instructions

Body

1 Cut 15cm (6in) of wire and pass 1 bead to the middle.
2 Thread and knit 1 bead.
3 Repeat row 2 six times.
4 Thread and knit 1 coloured bead for the head.
5 Trim wires for the antennae.

Wings

1 Cut 15cm (6in) of wire. Pass through bead below head.

Thread 20 beads each side.

2 Pass both ends of the wire through the same bead again. Twist to secure. Trim ends.
3 Cut a third length of wire. Pass through next bead down. Add 10 beads to each side.
4 Pass both ends of wire through the same bead again. Twist to secure. Trim off, or bend to form legs.

LARGE DRAGONFLY

This motif is made in the same way as the small dragonfly but larger beads make it look very different. It is 6cm (2¼in) across, and an older child should be able to make it.

Finished size
15 x 15cm (6 x 6in)

You will need...

Motif
- 41 gold 4mm round beads
- 21 blue/multi 4mm beads
- 28-gauge wire

Card
- White card 30 x 15cm (12 x 6in), folded
- Blue backing paper 13 x 13cm (5 x 5in)
- White wavy corrugated card 11 x 11cm (4¼ x 4¼in)
- Pearl blue dimensional paint
- Glue stick or double-sided adhesive tape
- Glue dots
- Daisy punch

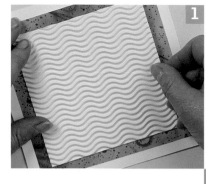

1 Layer and attach the blue backing paper and white wavy corrugated paper.

2 Attach the motif using a large glue dot.

3 Punch out flowers from matching backing paper. Glue to card.

4 Decorate the centre of the daisies and the corners of the card with dimensional paint.

Crafty touch

Treat corrugated card gently when cutting or attaching motifs, or the pattern may become squashed.

Threading instructions

Make in exactly the same way as the small dragonfly, using longer wires and larger beads. Twist to secure. Trim off, or bend to form legs.

BEE

This cute little bee is quick and easy to make, and a favourite with people of all ages and sexes.

Finished size
13.5 x 10cm (5¼ x 4in)

You will need...

Motif
- 62 silver embroidery beads
- 12 yellow embroidery beads
- 12 black embroidery beads
- 2 larger round black beads
- 34-gauge gold or silver wire

Card
- Mauve pearlized card 20 x 13.5cm (8 x 5¼in), folded
- White card 12.5 x 10cm (5 x 4in)
- Purple textured paper 12 x 9.5cm (4 x 3in)
- Creamy yellow textured paper 11.5 x 9cm (4½ x 3½in)
- Spare textured paper
- Yellow accent beads
- Green dimensional paint
- Double-sided adhesive tape
- Glue dot
- Daisy punch
- Small leaf punch

Crafty touch

Beads may vary in size even if they are the same make, so you may have to adjust the given number of beads.

Bee

1 Assemble and attach the paper and card. Punch 6 leaves with the leaf punch and glue on card. Draw stalks using green dimensional paint.

2 Punch three flowers from spare textured paper. Dot glue in the flower centres and sprinkle on accent beads (see p.15).

3 Attach the flowers using glue dots.

4 Attach the bee using a glue dot.

Threading instructions

1 Cut 20cm (8in) of wire. Pass 4 black beads to centre
2 Thread/knit 4 yellow beads.
3 Thread/knit 4 black beads.
4 Repeat row 2.
5 Repeat row 3.
6 Repeat row 2.
7 Thread 2 larger black beads. Trim ends for the antennae.

Wings
1 Cut 15cm (6in) of wire. Pass through first black row.

2 Thread 16 silver beads on one side. Pass through the first yellow row and leave.
3 Repeat step 2 for other side.
4 Cut 15cm (6in) of wire. Pass through next black row down.
5 Thread 15 silver beads on one side. Pass through the yellow row above.
6 Repeat step 5 for fourth wing.
7 Twist ends at the back. Trim, or twist to represent legs.

Step-by-Step Bead Cards

69

FLIGHTS OF FANTASY 1

Create stunning fantasy creatures by adding beaded bodies to ribbon.
This pretty motif on a ready-made embossed card would be perfect for
girls of all ages.

Finished size
15 x 10cm (6 x 4in)

You will need...

Motif
- 5 pink glossy beads
- 8-10 pink embroidery beads
- Silver wired netting ribbon
- 34-gauge wire
- Pink feather

Card
- Ready-made embossed card 15 x 10cm (6 x 4in)
- Glue dots

1 Gather 7cm (3in) of ribbon in the centre and wrap wire round to attach the wings.

2 Thread both wires through the second bead, then twist at the back to secure.

3 Move the end bead of the motif aside. Ease the end of the feather into the hole of the penultimate bead, trimming to fit if necessary.

4 Remove the feather and dab on a little glue. Insert the end in the bead again.

5 Attach the feather to the body, then attach to the ready-made embossed card using a glue dot.

Crafty Touch

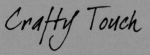

If the wings seem floppy, twist the wires together tightly at the back. Instead of adding tiny beads, just trim the wire antennae to length and curl round a cocktail stick

Threading instructions

1 Cut 21cm (8in) of wire. Pass 1 bead into the centre.

2 Bring the ends of the wire together. Pass both through another pink bead.

3 Thread and knit 1 bead.

4 Thread and knit 1 bead.

5 Thread 1 embroidery bead on a length of wire. Hold wire between finger and thumb. Pass through bead again.

6 Repeat to attach beads up length of wire.

7 Repeat for other antenna.

71

FLIGHTS OF FANTASY 2

This card was made in the same way as the previous project,
but using crystal beads and white ribbon and feather. The backing paper
is a beautiful thick embossed mulberry paper.

Finished size
20 x 10cm (8 x 4in)

You will need...

Motif
- Crystal beads
- White wired netting ribbon
- 34- or 28-gauge wire
- White feather

Card
- White card 20 x 10cm (8 x 8in), folded
- Gold card 17.5 x 7.5cm (7 x 3in)
- Terracotta embossed mulberry paper 17 x 6.5cm (6³/₄ x 2¹/₂in)
- Glue stick or double-sided adhesive tape
- Glue dot
- Fancy craft scissors with deckle edge

1 Gather 7cm (3in) of ribbon in the centre and wrap 15cm (6in) of wire round to secure.

2 Attach the body of the motif and fluff out the ribbon.

3 Wrap the ends of the antennae round a cocktail stick or the stem of a paintbrush to curl them.

4 Attach the mulberry paper to the gold card, then attach to the white base card.

5 Attach the butterfly to the centre of the card using a glue dot.

Crafty touch
Instead of cutting them off, leave the wire ends long and curl them to form legs.

Threading instructions
Follow the instructions for the previous project.

RIBBON BUTTERFLY

Skeleton leaves come in a beautiful assortment of colours.
Match or contrast the ribbon, and add a final touch with punched
flowers and gemstones.

Finished size
15 x 10cm (6 x 4in)

You will need...

Motif
- 5 pearl beads
- 2 cream embroidery beads
- 34- or 28-gauge wire
- Cream wired ribbon

Card
- 20 x 15cm (8 x 6in) white card, folded
- 2 skeleton leaves
- Parchment paper
- Gemstones
- Glue stick
- Glue dots
- Flower punch
- Edge punch

1 Attach the wings to the body as in the previous projects.

2 Punch the edge of the white card using a decorative edge punch.

3 Attach the skeleton leaves to the card using the glue stick.

4 Attach the butterfly using a glue dot. Punch out the flowers and glue in position, adding gemstones for the centres.

Crafty touch

The ribbon edges might fray, so trim at the last moment.

Threading instructions

Complete as for the previous project.

WINGED BEAUTIES

These two little motifs were made from tiny beads and
left-over pieces of wired ribbon.

Finished size

15 x 15cm (6 x 6in)

You will need...

Motif

- 4 beads for each butterfly
- Small pieces of ribbon

Card

- 30 x 15cm (12 x 6in) white card, folded
- 16 x 16cm (6¼ x 6¼in) pink floral vellum paper
- Ribbon
- Glue stick or double-sided adhesive tape
- Glue dots
- Fancy craft scissors with deckle edge

1 Attach the wings to the body using wire, as in previous projects.

2 Trim the pink vellum using fancy craft scissors.

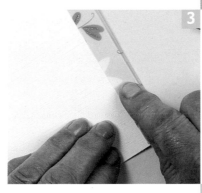

3 Place on the base card, fold the excess to the back, and attach.

4 Attach each butterfly to a flower on the front of the card. Tie ribbon to the card.

Crafty touch

Do not trim the ends of the ribbon until you are ready to attach them to the card, or they might fray.

Threading instructions

Make in exactly the same way as the body of the butterfly in the previous project, but with four beads instead of five.

More help with threading instructions

These diagrams should help you to understand some of the more intricate threading instructions used for the projects.

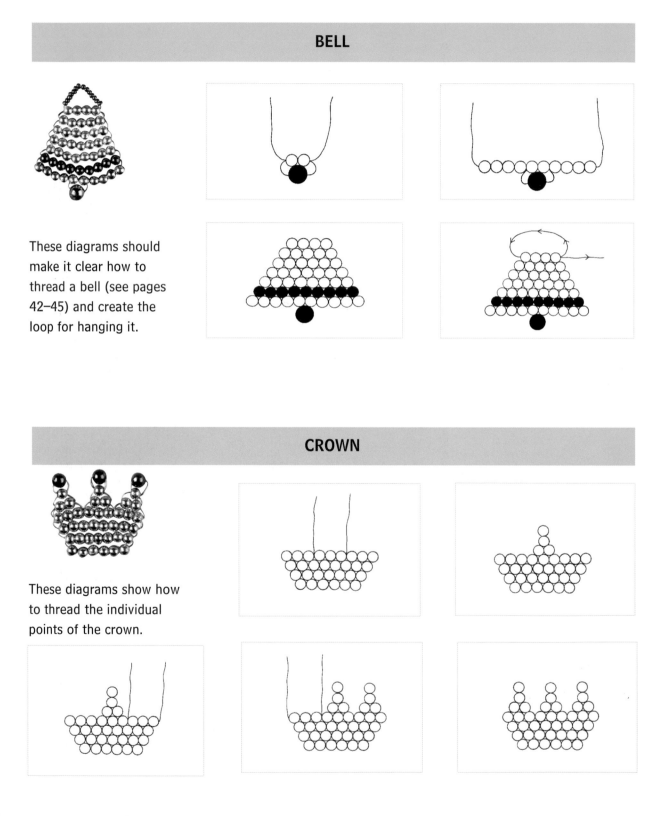

BELL

These diagrams should make it clear how to thread a bell (see pages 42–45) and create the loop for hanging it.

CROWN

These diagrams show how to thread the individual points of the crown.

BIRTHDAY CAKE

The diagram shows how to thread the wire through to make the candles.

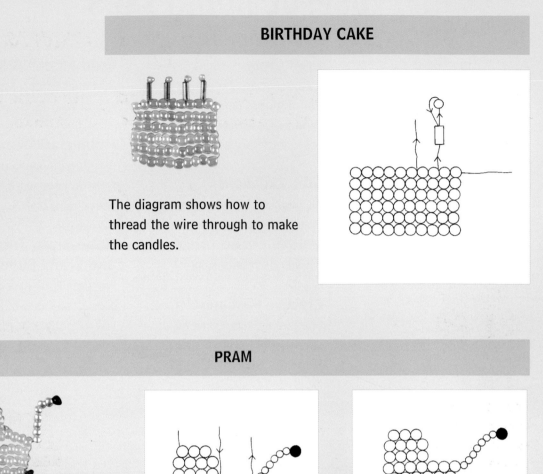

PRAM

Follow the diagram to thread the pram handle and wheels.

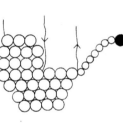
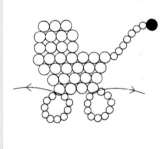

BUTTERFLY

Follow the diagrams to thread the wings of the butterfly.

USEFUL ADDRESSES

ArtyCrafty
9 Church Street,
Godalming, Surrey
GU7 1EQ / 01483 427133
www.artycraft.com
email: artycrafty@aol.com

The Craft Barn
9 East Grinstead Road,
Lingfield, Surrey
RH7 6EP / 01342 836097
www.craftbarn.co.uk

Craft Crazy
2 Barley Road, Thelwall,
Warrington, Cheshire
WA4 2EZ / 01925 263263
www.craftcrazy.co.uk

Craft Creations
4B Ingersoll House, Delamere
Road, Cheshunt, Herts
EN8 9HD / 01992 781900
www.craftcreations.com

Creative Pastimes
Boulthurst Farm, Pains Hill,
Limpsfield, Surrey
RH8 ORG / 01883 730033

Fred Aldous (CB01)
37 Lever Street, Manchester
M1 1LW / 08707 517301/2

Hobbicraft Dept. CB
40 Woodhouse Lane, Merrion
Centre, Leeds LS2 8LX
www.hobbicraft.co.uk

**Hobbycraft, The Arts
and Crafts Superstore**
For details of your nearest
store, call 0800 027 2387
www.hobbycraft.co.uk

INDEX